YOUR SANDWICH MADE IT!

Absolute Press

First published in 2006 by

Absolute Press
Scarborough House
29 James Street West
Bath BA1 2BT
Phone 44 (0) 1225 316013
Fax 44 (0) 1225 445836
E-mail info@absolutepress.co.uk
Website www.absolutepress.co.uk

Food Photography by Andy Davis
Design by Dialogue Marketing

A catalogue record of this book is available from the British Library

ISBN: 1904573576
ISBN 13: 9781904573579

Printed and bound by Lego, Italy

A BIG thank you

...to the thousands of people who contributed a sarnie recipe to our sandwich site

www.WillYourSandwichMakeIt.com

And a big round of applause to those who formed the upper crust and made it into the best sandwich book since sliced bread.

This is what we've SQUEEZED in!

Kiddies' Favourites 34

Gail Porter's sandwich
Mermaid's Mackerel Magic
Healthy Surprise
Tuna Cheese Bites

Kieran's Chinese Delight
Rule Britannia
Cheese, Carrot and Mayo

Odd But Excellent 42

Filly Fish Surprise
Sue Perkins' sandwich
Big Mumma Jumma Sandwich
Chicken Crazy
NY Pastrami Bagel

Toby Anstis' sandwich
Hawaiian Pizza-Style
Sandwich
God's Gift
Strawberry Fields Forever!

Feeling Exotic 50

Tamzin Outhwaite's sandwich
Fruity Salad Wrap
Orient Express
East Meets West

Steak Barm with Guacamole
Exotic Egg and Mayo doorstep
Tandoori Taste Temptation
Toasted Mediterranean Ciabatta

Winning Chef's Sandwich 57

Winning Sandwich 58

Fun At The Final 60

Making The Book

You know how you've always made that sandwich that's good enough to be SOLD?

The one you insist on allllways having. Your quirky preparation rituals. The great everyday sandwich for us to make and sell. Well we at Hellmann's went in search for that sandwich that tantalised the taste buds the most.

Thousands of sandwich connoisseurs submitted their fav, before a team of independent judges short-listed the recipes to 36. The semi-finalist recipes appeared in the Mail on Sunday in August and were put to the public vote. Before you could say "No mayo? No wayo!" 18 finalists went bread to bread in our live final for a chance to baguette one sandwich lover the chance for fame and fortune.

A few celebrity friends couldn't resist getting involved as well and we were only too happy to thank them by donating £500 each to charities close to their hearts.

And the result - the best recipe book since sliced bread.

However you like your sandwich, Hellmann's makes it.

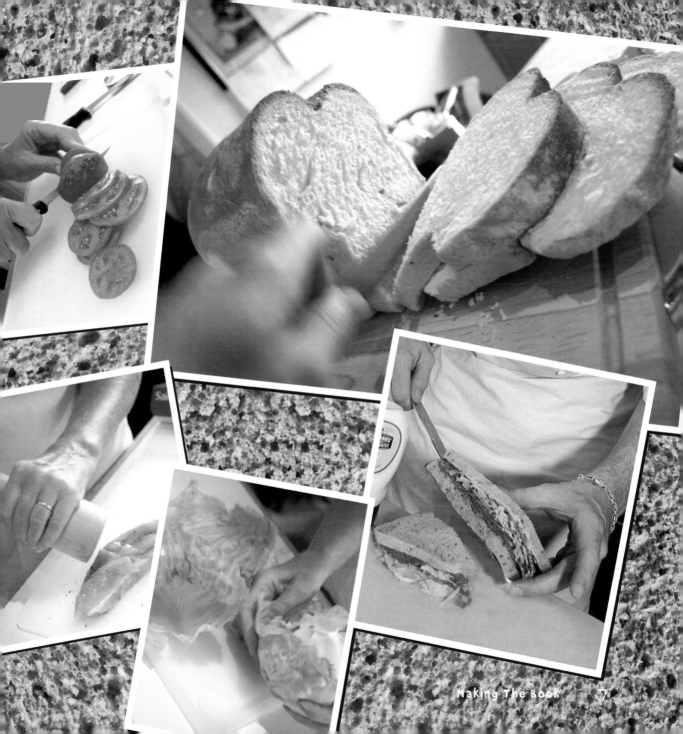

Silvana Franco- celebrity chef

Growing up in a large Italian family where daily life focussed round the hustle and bustle of the kitchen, cooking has always been a passion of mine. Like most people, I want tasty food that's quick and easy to make, which is why the Great British sandwich is a dish I never bore of reinventing. Whether you fancy a gourmet delight such as a black-olive and Feta ciabatta or a comforting bacon bite on sliced white, the variations are endless.

Evident from the culinary combinations in this book - you create the sandwich - Hellmann's Mayonnaise makes it. This cookbook showcases mouth-watering recipes, ideas and tips to liven up any loaf, roll or wrap. It captures the spirit of quality food prepared with genuine passion, for the people, by the people.

SILVANA'S

- master class -

1. Take your sandwich out of the fridge 30 minutes before you eat it. Bread tastes fresher and has a much better texture at room temperature than when cold.

2. For a flavour-packed twist to your sandwich, try livening up the Hellmann's Mayonnaise by mashing in some herbs or a pinch of dried chilli flakes.

3. Self-assembly sandwiches can make your lunch box more exciting. Try packing the bread roll, filling and extras such as pickles separately then you can have a mini picnic at your desk.

4. Rather than eating your way through the same loaf day after day, buy a varied selection of different rolls and keep them in the freezer and pull out the one you fancy in the morning. Bread doesn't take long to defrost and frozen rolls can be sawed through with a small serrated knife if you're really in a hurry.

5. Get organised and prepare your fillings the night before but do not make the whole sandwich - unless you like them soggy. Just quickly put together before you leave in the morning.

Lunchbox Inspirations

The perfect moveable feast:

a transportable sandwich that can be wrapped
easily and eaten anywhere - it should be the
envy of hungry onlookers wherever you go.

Ingredients

2 slices of thick, white good quality bread
Hellmann's Light Mayonnaise
2 slices lean, thick cut smoked bacon, well-done
a few rocket leaves
3-4 slices creamy French Brie
chunky mango chutney, to spread

How you make it

Spread one slice of the bread with Hellmann's Light Mayonnaise and top with the smoked bacon. Add the rocket leaves and the slices of creamy Brie. Spread another slice of bread with the mango chutney, pile it all up and devour contentedly.

The BBMM (Bacon, Brie and Mango Mayo)

created by
Sue Price-Whittle

Suzanne Shaw

MY SANDWICH

"A simple chicken sandwich - use your imagination and add whatever herbs or spices you feel like to bump up the flavours. Tarragon, basil, mint or cayenne pepper would be good."

Ingredients

roast chicken pieces mixed with herbs or spices of your choice
salad leaves
2 slices wheat-free bread
a little Hellmann's Extra Light Mayonnaise as a finishing touch

How you make it

Place the slices of roast chicken on a piece of wheat-free bread. Sprinkle your desired herbs and spices on top of the chicken and then layer some salad leaves on top. To finish, spread a little Hellmann's Extra Light Mayonnaise on the other slice of bread and close to seal your sandwich.

chosen donation: NSPCC

Registered Charity Number 216401

Jamaican... Lunch

created by
Linda christie

Ingredients

1 cooked chicken breast coated in
   Jamaican Jerk Spices
cucumber, diced
iceberg lettuce, shredded
Hellmann's Real Mayonnaise
pitta bread, heated and split

How you make it

Chop the jerk chicken into bite-size pieces
and add the diced cucumber, the shredded
iceberg lettuce plus a good dollop Hellmann's
Real Mayonnaise. Mix together well and
spoon into the hot envelope of pitta bread.

SILVANA'S sandwich

Satay chicken wraps

"This is a fabulous way to use up
cold leftover chicken and is ideal
for those who don't like too much
bread with their sandwich. The
satay sauce has a great texture."

Ingredients

Some Hellmann's Real Mayonnaise
1 tablespoon crunchy
   peanut butter
splash of soy sauce
1 flour tortilla
1 iceberg lettuce leaf, rolled up
   and shredded
cold roast chicken, roughly torn
1 carrot, coarsely grated
handful of salad cress
wedge of fresh lime

The JOEy Special
(my nickname)

created by Julian Roger

Ingredients
white baguette
Hellmann's Real Mayonnaise
red onion, sliced
cucumber, sliced
tomato, sliced
cos lettuce
a slice of mature cheddar cheese
a slice of ham
English mustard, to spread

How you make it
Spread Hellmann's Real Mayonnaise on both sides of a halved baguette. Add the red onion, cucumber, tomato and lettuce to the base. Place the cheddar cheese on top and top with the ham. To finish the Joey Special simply spread with English mustard and tuck in.

How you make it
Mix together the Hellmann's Real Mayonnaise, peanut butter and soy sauce. Spread onto the tortilla. Pile on the lettuce, chicken, carrot and salad cress. Season with salt, pepper and a squeeze of fresh lime. Roll up tightly then wrap in a paper napkin or greaseproof paper. For a pretty finish, roll again in a sheet of coloured tissue paper, twisting the ends together like a party cracker.

Ingredients

Red pepper and onion,
caramelised (see below)
mixed herbs (say
   thyme and oregano)
brown sugar,
   to sprinkle
Hellmann's Mayonnaise
   with Olive Oil
white sub roll
grilled chicken, sliced

Italian Sub

How you make it

Dice some red pepper and
onion and gently fry in butter
with the mixed herbs until softened. Add a sprinkle of brown sugar and continue
to fry for a few more minutes until nicely caramelised. Spread some Hellmann's
Mayonnaise with Olive Oil on a split sub roll and then layer on the sliced, grilled
chicken breast. Finish with the caramelised onion and pepper.

inspired by
Dana Lewis

The Food of Love

Chicken Pesto Mayo

created by
Andrew Crowther

Ingredients

1 chicken breast, grilled
Hellmann's Light Mayonnaise
2 slices white wholemeal bread
Parmesan
rocket leaves
tomato, sliced
pesto, homemade or bought

How you make it

Spread some Hellmann's Light Mayonnaise on a slice of white wholemeal bread and add the grilled chicken. Grate over some Parmesan, add a few rocket leaves and some tomato slices. Mix the pesto with more Hellmann's and spread on a second slice of the bread. Sandwich together - and hey Pesto!

Ingredients

2 slices white bread
butter, for spreading
green salad leaves
rasher of smoked bacon, grilled
1 avocado, sliced
lemon juice
Hellmann's Real Mayonnaise with added Dijon Mustard
1 tablespoon of medium-sized cooked prawns, shelled

How you make it

Butter two slices of white bread and add a layer of green salad leaves. Tear the rasher of smoked bacon into pieces and mix with the chopped avocado, a squeeze of lemon juice and Hellmann's Mayonnaise with added Dijon Mustard. Add the prawns and spread over the salad. Top with the second slice of bread and get munching.

created by
chris Hulbert

wholesome Heroes

For those with a hearty Hellmann's outlook -

and a healthy appetite - choose from a bunch of mouthwatering sandwich ideas, all of which are nutritious, delicious and satisfying.

Ingredients

juicy prawns, cooked and shelled
a touch of tomato purée and Hellmann's Real
  Mayonnaise, mixed together
2 slices of Granary bread

How you make it

Put the prawns in a bowl with delicious
Hellmann's Real Mayonnaise and a touch
of tomato purée. Make sure the
prawns are covered with the
mixture and then pile it onto
one slice of bread. Finish by
placing the other slice of
bread on top, carefully
ensuring that none of
the prawns spill out.

Sally Gunnell

"Either cook the prawns yourself for
maximum freshness or seek out just
cooked ones - the result will be worth it."

 chosen donation: childline

Registered Charity Number 1003758

Wholegrain Happiness

Ingredients

prawns, cooked and peeled
fresh coriander, chopped
freshly ground black pepper
lime juice
2 slices of thickly cut wholegrain bloomer
Hellmann's Extra Light Mayonnaise.
lettuce, shredded

How you make it

Mix together the prawns, chopped coriander, black pepper and lime juice. Take the two slices of wholegrain bloomer and spread both with Hellmann's Extra Light Mayonnaise. Top one slice with shredded lettuce and then pile on the prawn mix.

created by
Karen Huxtable

Created by Andrea Moro

Dr. Feelgood

Ingredients
wasabi paste
tortilla wrap
Hellmann's Real Mayonnaise
cooked ham, sliced
fresh button mushrooms, sliced
roasted red peppers, skinned, deseeded and
   cut into strips
watercress

How you make it
Mix some Hellmann's Real Mayonnaise with a
little wasabi paste (be careful, it is
seriously hot!) and spread on the tortilla.
Add the ham, mushrooms and roasted red
peppers. Finally add a handful of
watercress, then roll your wrap and cut
diagonally in half.

Indian Delight
Ingredients
Some Hellmann's Extra
   Light Mayonnaise
1 small tablespoon natural yogurt
$1/2$ teaspoon mint sauce
coriander, chopped
cucumber, skinned and chopped
spring onion, sliced
wholemeal pitta bread
tandoori chicken pieces
sun-dried tomatoes, chopped

How you make it
Make up a raita by mixing the Hellmann's
Extra Light Mayonnaise with the natural
yogurt, mint sauce, coriander, cucumber and
spring onion. Spread the inside of the wholemeal
pitta envelope with the raita, add the tandoori
chicken pieces and some chopped sun-dried tomato.

chris Hoy

"Rich and satisfying - be sure to be generous with your twists of freshly ground black pepper."

MY SANDWICH

Ingredients
good quality canned tuna
Hellmann's Real Mayonnaise
freshly ground black pepper
crusty white roll
cucumber, sliced
avocado, thinly sliced

How you make it
Mix some tuna with a big dollop of Hellmann's Real Mayonnaise and some freshly ground black pepper. Fill a crusty white roll with the mixture and add the cucumber and sliced avocado.

chosen donation:
children's Leukaemia charity

Registered Charity Number 298405

created by
Lilu O'Dedra

The Green Goddess

Ingredients

2 slices of olive and multi-seed bread
extra soft, slow roasted sugar-basted chicken breasts, sliced
lots of coriander, freshly chopped
baby spinach leaves
basil leaves
cos lettuce leaves
iceberg lettuce leaves
rich red tomatoes, sliced
olives, chopped
celery, diced
Hellmann's Mayonnaise with Olive Oil

created by
Linsay Bryans

How you make it

Mix the chicken breast and Hellmann's Mayonnaise with Olive Oil and place on one slice of the bread. Sprinkle on the chopped coriander leaves, then add the baby spinach, basil, cos and iceberg leaves and top with the tomatoes, olives and celery. Top with the second slice of bread to finish off this brilliant Mediterranean inspired sandwich.

created by
Paula Kay Godfrey

Salmon Sublime

Ingredients

lemon juice
paprika
chilli powder
Hellmann's Light Mayonnaise
fresh poached salmon, flaked
tortilla wrap
avocado, thinly sliced
cherry tomatoes, chopped
watercress or rocket

How you make it

Mix a squeeze of lemon juice and a pinch of paprika and chilli into the Hellmann's Light Mayonnaise. Add the salmon and spread on a tortilla wrap. Top with the avocado, cherry tomatoes and watercress or rocket. Roll it up and eat. Sublime!

Sweet chilli prawn pitta

"Prawn and mayonnaise is a timeless combination but it can be a little short on excitement. I've given it a new lease of life here with some sweet chilli sauce and peppery wild rocket leaves. Delicious"

Ingredients

Some Hellmann's Real Mayonnaise
1 tablespoon sweet chilli sauce
1 white pitta
150g cooked king prawns
few thin slices red onion
handful wild rocket

How you make it

Ripple together the mayonnaise and sweet chilli sauce but don't blend completely. Split open the pitta and fill with the prawns, red onion and rocket. Top with the dressing then wrap and pack.

SILVANA'S sandwich

Sumptuous salmon scramble

Ingredients

For the scrambled eggs:
1 egg
paprika
splash of skimmed milk
freshly ground black pepper

Hellmann's Light Mayonnaise
2 pieces of granary bread
1 leaf of chinese lettuce
smoked salmon

created by Nick Shaw

How you make it

The perfect sandwich for those who do lunch! Scramble an egg with a sprinkle of paprika, black pepper and a splash of skimmed milk. Spread Hellmann's Light Mayonnaise on the slices of granary bread and add a chinese lettuce leaf and a layer of smoked salmon to the base of one. Spoon on the scrambled egg and sandwich together.

Weekend Hungerbusters

Now these are recipes to challenge even the hungriest of sandwich lovers!

Bulging bagels, bursting baguettes, packed paninis, all crammed with flavourful fillings. Hellmann's Hungerbusters take no hostages and are guaranteed to satisfy even the most demanding of appetites. Now eat on...

Amour

Ingredients
roasted chicken pieces
smoked ham
back bacon
Hellmann's Real
Mayonnaise
butter, for spreading
2 slices of white bread
lettuce leaves
hot portabello mushrooms,
lightly fried in garlic
  and butter
red onion, thinly sliced
Feta cheese

How you make it
Butter the slices of bread and pile
some roasted chicken pieces mixed
with smoked ham, bacon and
Hellmann's Real Mayonnaise onto the
base of one. Add the lettuce leaves,
sliced mushrooms, red onion and
crumbled Feta and sandwich together.

created by Alex Langford

Jeremy Edwards

MY SANDWICH

"The extra kick of hot English mustard adds a fiery twist to a well loved classic. Super tasty, super healthy!"

Ingredients
canned tuna
Hellmann's Light Mayonnaise
hot English mustard
wholemeal pitta, toasted
1 tomato, sliced
cucumber, sliced
sweetcorn
cheddar cheese

How you make it
Mix the canned tuna with Hellmann's Light Mayonnaise and a touch of English mustard. Stuff this mixture into the toasted pitta. Squeeze the tomato, cucumber and sweetcorn in the pitta and grate the cheese on top.

chosen donation: PDSA
Registered Charity Number 208217

Goats' cheese, Roasted Pepper and Basil Panini

Ingredients

1 red bell pepper, roasted in olive oil
1 yellow bell pepper, roasted in olive oil
goats' cheese
3-4 teaspoons basil
1 panini
Hellmann's Light Mayonnaise

How you make it

Spread a layer of goats' cheese on the panini top with strips of the roasted red and yellow peppers and fresh basil. Add some Hellmann's Light Mayonnaise. Toast under the grill.

Ingredients

honey and mustard pork sausages
1 medium onion, sliced
olive oil
white baguette
butter for spreading
Hellmann's Mayonnaise with
    added Dijon Mustard

How you make it

cook the sausages, while at the same time warming the baguette and frying the onion in olive oil until soft and caramelised. Spread the baguette with butter and Hellmann's Mayonnaise with added Dijon Mustard, pile on the sausages and onions.

Breakfast Bangers!

Roast Beef Gut-Buster

Ingredients
1 bagel, split in half
Hellmann's Real Mayonnaise
roast beef, sliced
cheddar cheese, sliced
barbecue sauce

How you make it
Fill the bagel with Hellmann's Real Mayonnaise, the roast beef, cheddar cheese and some barbecue sauce. Simple as that!

Created by
Sharon Page

Created by Jodie Lever

Created by
Melanie Smith

warm spiced Roast Pork, stuffing and Apple Baguette

Ingredients

leftover Spiced Roast Pork, roasted with
dried chilli flakes, oregano, basil, fennel
seeds and rosemary (possibly from roast
lunch the day before).
baguette
freshly-made Bramley apple sauce or best
shop bought
sage and onion stuffing
gravy
Hellmann's Real Mayonnaise

How you make it

Slice the leftover spiced roast pork and warm
thoroughly in the oven. Spread a
baguette with the sage and onion
stuffing mixed with some gravy
and Hellmann's Real Mayonnaise.
Place the warm pork in the
sandwich and finally add the
apple sauce.

created by Junho Scott

Fillet Steakwich

Ingredients

2 slices white bread
some onion, sliced
5 chestnut mushrooms
butter, to cook and 1 clove garlic, crushed
1 fillet steak
white wine (optional)
2 tbsp single cream (optional)
horseradish sauce
large dollop Hellmann's Real Mayonnaise
rocket

How you make it

Toast the bread. Sauté the onion and chestnut mushrooms
in butter with the garlic. Remove. Fry the fillet steak. When
cooked to your liking, slice diagonally. Deglaze the pan with white
wine, add the onions and mushrooms and single cream and bubble up the
sauce. Spread the horseradish sauce and Hellmann's Real Mayonnaise on the toast
and pile the steak and mushroom and onion sauce on top. Finish the sandwich with some
rocket leaves. You have just made one of the best steak sandwiches in the world!

classic Parma ciabatta

"A classic combo of Italian ham and cheese paired together with fresh, fragrant basil. This is also very tasty when toasted."

Ingredients

1 large ciabatta roll or ½ a regular-sized loaf
1 tablespoon sun dried tomato paste or red pesto
Some Hellmann's Real Mayonnaise

3 slices Parma ham
5 baby Mozzarella balls or 3 thick slices of mozzarella
handful fresh basil
splash of Tabasco

How you make it

Split open the ciabatta and spread one side with the paste or pesto and the other with Hellmann's Real Mayonnaise. Fill with the ham, Mozzarella and basil adding a splash of Tabasco if you like chilli. Serve with a simple side salad or toast until the ciabatta is golden and the mozzarella oozes over the side and eat whilst warm.

created by
Gareth Watt

SILVANA'S sandwich

Kiddies' Favourites

Sandwich recipes guaranteed to put a smile on even the grumpiest of children - fun, colourful, tasty and wholesome. Everything a hungry child and a loving parent could want.

Ingredients

Hellmann's Real Mayonnaise
2 slices wholemeal bread
Brie
tomato, sliced
lettuce

How you make it

Spread a generous amount of Hellmann's
Real Mayonnaise onto both pieces of
wholemeal bread. Place a few pieces of
creamy Brie on one side of the bread. Layer
the tomatoes and lettuce on top of the Brie and
sandwich together the pieces of bread. To finish,
cut off the crusts and cut into a heart shape.

MY SANDWICH

Gail Porter

"A deliciously cheesy sandwich in the shape of
a heart - one for the romantics out there!"

chosen donation:
ActionAid

Registered Charity Number 27264198

Ingredients

1 fillet smoked mackerel, flaked
Hellmann's Real Mayonnaise
baguette
2 cherry tomatoes
1 stick celery
slices of cucumber, halved
1 grated carrot

How you make it

Kids will love this. Mix the flaked mackerel fillet with Hellmann's Real Mayonnaise. Fill an open baguette with the mixture. Give some character to the filling with the addition of two cherry tomatoes as eyes, celery for the mouth, cucumber slices as the scales and some grated carrot to look like a mermaid's tail.

created by Bernadette Oliver

Mermaid's Mackerel Magic

Tuna cheese Bites

Ingredients
canned tuna
Hellmann's Real Mayonnaise
2 slices white bread
cheddar cheese, grated
cucumber, sliced
raisins

How you make it
Mix the canned tuna with Hellmann's Real Mayonnaise and spread on a piece of bread. Sprinkle with the grated cheddar cheese and top with the remaining slice of bread. Cut into fish shapes and add cucumber to resemble a fin and raisins for the eyes.

created by Bridget Betts

Healthy Surprise

Ingredients
Hellmann's Extra
  Light Mayonnaise
2 slices white bread
cheese, grated
apple, sliced
raisins

How you make it
Spread Hellmann's Extra Light Mayonnaise on one slice of bread. Sprinkle the grated cheese on top and add the sliced apple and a handful of raisins. Top with the second slice of bread and cut into triangles.

created by catherine chapman

Ingredients

tortilla wrap
tomato sauce
shredded lettuce
hot chinese chicken,
  cut into pieces
carrot, freshly-grated
Hellmann's Extra Light Mayonnaise

Kieran's chinese Delight

How you make it

This is one your older children will really like. Warm the tortilla wrap and spread it with tomato sauce. Lay the lettuce at one end and add a few chinese chicken pieces and the finely grated carrot. Top with Hellmann's Extra Light Mayonnaise, then roll up the wrap and slice diagonally.

inspired by Kieran Duffy

Ingredients

Hellmann's Light Mayonnaise
blue food colouring
2 slices white bread
strawberry jam

How you make it

Mix some Hellmann's Light Mayonnaise with a tiny amount
of blue food colouring and spread on to two pieces of
white bread. Add a layer of strawberry jam and sandwich
together. Cut into triangles so that you can clearly see
the red, white and blue layers. Very patriotic!

Rule Britannia

Created by Julie Thomson

inspired by
Alex Mann and
created by
mum, Andrea
(with a bit of
help from dad!)

cheese, carrot and Mayo

Ingredients
cheese, finely grated
carrot finely grated
Hellmann's Light Mayonnaise
2 slices of seeded bread

How you make it
Mix the carrot and cheese with Hellmann's Light
Mayonnaise and sandwich between the two slices of bread.
Simple, but bound to be popular with the little ones.

Odd

But Excellent

Why should everything in life be predictable?

The surprisingly brilliant recipes in this oddball chapter prove just how great the unexpected in a sandwich can be. Although one thing, of course, always brings it all together - the reassuring ingredient of Hellmann's Mayonnaise!

Filly Fish Surprise

created by
Phil Eldred

Ingredients

butter for spreading
poppy seed roll, split
wild rocket
fresh mint, finely chopped
poached salmon, flaked
freshly ground black pepper
Hellmann's Extra Light
  Mayonnaise
raspberries, halved

How you make it

Butter the roll and create a bed of
rocket and mint. Mix the salmon
with Hellmann's Extra Light
Mayonnaise and place on top of
the rocket and mint. Add a layer
of fresh raspberries before
replacing the top of the roll.
Fruit and fish can make a
surprisingly fantastic combo.

Ingredients

canned tuna
gherkins, chopped
Hellmann's Real
  Mayonnaise
tomato ketchup
capers
lemon juice
2 slices of white
bread

How you make it

Empty some canned tuna into a bowl and mix in some chopped gherkins. Spoon in a big dollop of Hellmann's Real Mayonnaise and add a generous squeeze of tomato ketchup. Add a few capers and a big squeeze of fresh lemon juice. Pile this mixture onto one slice of soft white bread and top with the other.

Sue Perkins

"The sharpness of the gherkins and the capers helps cut through the oiliness of the tuna and marries perfectly with the rich sweetness of the ketchup and the Hellmann's Real Mayonnaise."

 chosen donation:
Macmillan cancer Support

Registered Charity Number 261017

MY SANDWICH

BIG Mumma Jumma Sandwich

Ingredients

2 slices of crusty white bread
butter for spreading
iceberg lettuce
Hellmann's Real Mayonnaise
smoked salmon, thinly sliced
tiger prawns
beef tomatoes, sliced
watercress
lemon juice

created by
Anita Stollery

How you make it

Butter the two chunky slices of crusty bread
and layer the bottom slice with iceberg lettuce
and Hellmann's Real Mayonnaise. Add the smoked
salmon, scatter with tiger prawns and a layer
of the tomato slices. cover with watercress and
sprinkle with lemon juice.

chicken Crazy

created by
Maja Saran

Ingredients

pine nuts, roasted
cold plain grilled chicken
Hellmann's Real Mayonnaise
green seedless grapes, halved
baguette

How you make it

Tear the cooked chicken breast into bite-sized
pieces and stir in Hellmann's Real Mayonnaise plus
some halved green seedless grapes. cut a section
of baguette and slice almost in half. Fill with the
chicken mix and sprinkle with the pine nuts.

NY pastrami BAGEL

"The true taste of New York City, pastrami is a cured beef and is often used with pickles. The mustard mayo adds the finishing touch."

Ingredients

Some Hellmann's Real Mayonnaise
1 tablespoon American yellow mustard
1 bagel
thin pastrami slices
1 slice Gruyère or Jarlsberg cheese
1 large dill pickle, sliced

SILVANA'S sandwich

How you make it

Mix together the mayonnaise and mustard.
Split open the bagel and spread both sides with the mustard mayo.
Arrange the pastrami slices and then the cheese on the bottom half of the bagel. Lay the sliced pickle on top and sandwich on the lid. Secure in place with a short bamboo skewer then wrap in waxed paper.

"A quintessential west country sandwich that uses a delicious and unusual smoked cheddar."

Ingredients

2 slices of Granary bread, thickly-cut
a good dollop of Hellmann's Real Mayonnaise
smoked cheddar cheese, cut into chunky slices
tomato, sliced
cucumber, sliced

How you make it

Smear the bread with the Hellmann's Real Mayonnaise. Place the chunky slices of smoked cheddar cheese on the bread and then layer with the slices of tomatoes and cucumber.

Toby Anstis

chosen donation: childline

Registered Charity Number 1003758

Hawaiian Pizza-style Sandwich

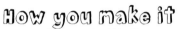

Ingredients

2 slices white bread
butter for spreading
tomato, sliced
cheddar cheese, grated
Ham, sliced
canned pineapple chunks or slices
sweetcorn (optional)
Hellmann's Real Mayonnaise

How you make it

Butter one slice of bread and add layers of tomato, cheddar cheese and ham. Place the canned pineapple pieces on top of the ham along with some sweetcorn. Spread Hellmann's Real Mayonnaise on the other slice of bread to finish off the sandwich.

created by Kevin Tran

God's Gift

created by Ian

Ingredients

streaky bacon
butter for spreading
baguette
cheese
Danish salami
lettuce
Hellmann's Light
  Mayonnaise

How you make it

Fry the streaky bacon. Butter the baguette and add a layer of cheese, some Danish salami, then more cheese. Add the warm bacon and some Hellmann's Light Mayonnaise. Finish with a final layer of crisp, crunchy lettuce - heavenly!

created by Nikki Marsh

Strawberry Fields Forever!

Ingredients

Mozzarella cheese
2 slices of poppy seed bloomer
strawberries, diced
mango, diced
Hellmann's Real Mayonnaise
basil leaves

How you make it

create a layer of Mozzarella cheese on one slice of the bloomer. Stir the strawberries and mango into some Hellmann's Real Mayonnaise. Spread the mix onto the cheese layer. Add some shredded basil leaves before sealing with another slice of bread.

Feeling Exotic

Fantastic fillings from far flung cuisines

proving that variety really is the spice of life. Take inspiration from your travels and experiment with the world's most exotic spices and flavourings to give your Hellmann's hit a delicious taste of the world.

Tamzin Outhwaite

"A wonderfully healthy and very tasty filling, sandwiched between traditional braided bread."

Ingredients

2 slices cholla bread, thickly cut
Hellmann's Light Mayonnaise
avocado, sliced
lemon juice
freshly ground black pepper
smoked salmon

How you make it

Spread the slices of cholla with Hellmann's Light Mayonnaise. Add some sliced avocado to one piece of bread. Squeeze some fresh lemon juice and some freshly ground black pepper on the smoked salmon and place this on top of the avocado. Top with the second slice of bread.

 chosen donation:
The James Baldwin Trust

Registered Charity Number 1114389

created by
Kelly Forbes

Fruity Salad Wrap

Ingredients

tortilla wrap
Hellmann's Extra Light
  Mayonnaise
strong Cheddar cheese,
  grated
mixed peppers, diced

rocket
onion, diced
mango chutney
a dash of smoked paprika
freshly ground black pepper
salad and cherry tomatoes,
  to serve

How you make it

Spread half the tortilla wrap with Hellmann's Extra Light
Mayonnaise. Lay on the Cheddar, chopped mixed peppers,
rocket, onion and mango chutney. Sprinkle with smoked
paprika and black pepper. Roll the wrap, tucking the ends in,
cut in half and serve with salad and cherry tomatoes.

Orient Express

Created by
Adrian Sleeman

Ingredients

Hellmann's Light Mayonnaise
Thai green curry paste
2 slices of white toast
chinese marinated chicken
  breast, sliced
spring onion, cut into strips
fresh ginger, cut into strips
red chilli, de-seeded and chopped
fresh coriander
lime juice

How you make it

For an exotic and delicious taste of the orient, mix Hellmann's Light Mayonnaise with a little Thai green curry paste and spread generously on two slices of white toast. Lay the sliced marinated chinese chicken onto the base and top with the spring onion, ginger, chopped red chilli and fresh coriander. Add a squeeze of lime juice and close with second slice of toast.

East Meets West

Ingredients

2 slices doorstep Granary bread
butter for spreading
Hellmann's Mayonnaise with
  Olive Oil
1 dessertspoon houmous
½ teaspoon mint sauce
1 tablespoon of
  cooked couscous
2 crisp cos lettuce leaves
2 slices beef tomato
2 slices of boned and rolled
leg of lamb, cooked pink or
  to your liking

How you make it

Butter the Granary bread. Mix the Hellmann's Mayonnaise with Olive Oil with the houmous and mint sauce and spread over both slices. Add a layer of couscous, a few cos lettuce leaves, the tomato slices and the lamb. Then simply sandwich together for a great taste fusion.

created by
christine Wren

Steak Barn with Guacamole

created by
caroline
Welding

Ingredients

large crunchy
  barn cake
butter, for spreading
sweet chilli sauce
Hellmann's Real
  Mayonnaise
sirloin steak
steak seasoning
oil

guacamole, freshly
  made or best
  shop bought
tomato, sliced
mixed salad leaves
red onion, sliced

How you make it

cut the barn cake in half and butter both sides. Spread the sweet chilli sauce on the base and Hellmann's Real Mayonnaise on the top. Season and grill the steak to your liking and then slice and place on top of the chilli sauce. Add the guacamole, tomato, salad leaves, red onion and top off with the barn.

EXOTIC EGG and mayo DOORSTEP

"This sandwich is particularly good made with sesame and onion seed-crusted Greek bread but any thickly sliced country loaf will do just fine"

SILVANA'S sandwich

Ingredients

1 large egg
Some Hellmann's
    Real Mayonnaise
2 spring onions, thinly sliced
2 thick slices of bread

small knob of butter
1/2 small avocado, sliced
25g feta, crumbled
fresh coriander leaves
packet of salted
crisps, to serve

How you make it

Cook the egg in a small pan of boiling water for exactly 8 minutes. Cool under running water then shell and mash with the Hellmann's Real Mayonnaise. Mix in the spring onions and some black pepper. Butter the bread and arrange the avocado on one slice. Spoon on the egg mixture then scatter over the feta and coriander leaves. Sandwich on the remaining slice of bread, pressing down firmly. Halve the sandwich and pack into a lunch box.

Tandoori Taste Temptation

Ingredients

Hellmann's Real Mayonnaise
mango chutney
cucumber, sliced
spring onion, sliced
little gem lettuce, shredded
2 slices of white bread
tandoori chicken breast, sliced

How you make it

Mix Hellmann's Real Mayonnaise with some mango chutney and spread on one slice of the bread. Add the spring onion, cucumber, gem lettuce and pile on top of the mayo mix. Lastly, add the slices of tandoori chicken and enjoy.

created by
Philip Penrith

winning chef's sandwich

Those cheeky chefs wanted to get in on the sandwich act too... so we organised a sandwich competition just for them!

Roast to go

Lawrence Keogh – Head chef, Roast Restaurant, Borough Market, London

The sandwich is named 'Hellmann's Roast to Go' following the opening of the Roast restaurant's new luxury sandwich stall in Borough market - Roast To Go. The inspiration for the recipe came from the time when Roast Head Chef Lawrence Keogh used to work at London's world famous Berkeley Hotel. At the end of each shift the German chef would make him a similar sandwich and ever since it has been a favourite of Lawrence's.

Ingredients

2 slices of crusty white bread,
rare roast beef, cut into thick slices
pastrami slices
red onion, sliced
iceberg lettuce
ketchup
seasoning
Hellmann's Real Mayonnaise

How you make it

Simply lay the pastrami and beef slices on a slice of the bread, add seasoning and layer with onion, a good squirt of ketchup and the lettuce. Finish with a good dollop of Hellmann's Real Mayonnaise.

WINNER
WINNER
YOUR
SANDWICH
MADE IT!

created by Marie Hubbard

Drum-roll please...
and the winner is...

Toasted Mediterranean-ciabatta

Ingredients

1 Mozzarella cheese, shredded
3 black olives, chopped
3 sun-dried tomatoes
extra virgin olive oil
1 ciabatta, cut in half
1 garlic clove, cut in half
Hellmann's Light Mayonnaise
small handful of basil leaves
5 slices of Milano salami
1 red pepper, charred
small handful of baby spinach leaves

How you make it

To the shredded Mozzarella, add the black olives and sun-dried tomatoes, and mix with some Hellmann's Light Mayonnaise. Drizzle olive oil over the ciabatta and lightly toast. Rub the halves of garlic on the toasted bread for flavour. Place the fresh basil leaves, the salami and the grilled Mozzarella mixture on one slice of the ciabatta. Add the spinach leaves and the slices of charred red pepper and top with the lid.

Fun At The Final

Sandwiched between celebrity guests Gail Porter, Mark Durden-Smith, Keith Chegwin, chef Silvana Franco and sandwich connoisseur Philip Brown, many of the competition's top 36 entrants gathered for a glittering affair in London in August.

The final sandwiches went bread to bread in a star-studded showbiz event. Imagine the tension, the excitement, the atmosphere you could cut with a knife. Whose Hellmann's Sandwich Would Make It?

After some serious taste testing, deliberating and sandwich shenanigans our panel of judges crowned the Toasted Mediterranean ciabatta as the competition's winner. As if seeing her creation sat on the shelves of her local supermarket wasn't enough, sandwich supremo Marie Hubbard is guaranteed at least 10k as a royalty payment on sales of her sandwich!

Our judges also deemed that all three finalists in the kiddies' favourites section (Tuna Cheese Bites, Mermaid's Mackerel Magic and Cheese, Carrot and Mayo) should each win £1,000 for their child's school as they simply couldn't choose a winner!
All in all the day was a cut above the rest.